A Culture of Quality

A Reflection on Practice

RON BERGER

Third edition

©2019 by EL Education. All rights reserved.

EL Education

247 West 35th St., 8th Floor
New York, NY 10001
212-239-4455

Design by Mike Kelly

This book features illustrations by a first grade student at
ANSER Charter School in Boise, Idaho. To view these and
other examples of high-quality student work, please visit
modelsofexcellence.ELeducation.org.

CONTENTS

A Culture of Quality: A Reflection on Practice

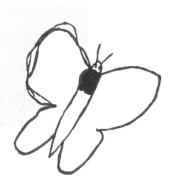

PREFACE

Reflecting on A Culture of Quality

IT'S BEEN TWENTY-FIVE YEARS since I wrote this small book. Some parts of my life have not changed at all. I still live on top of a hill overlooking a farm, in a small house I built with my family, hand-crafted out of local wood and stone. I still live in the tiny rural town where I was a public school teacher for decades. Almost every adult in my town is my former student.

I am still immensely proud of my students. My nurse is my former student. My plumber is my former student. The volunteer fire department members are my former students. The test scores they got in sixth grade no longer matter to me, but I care deeply about their commitment to quality, courage, and compassion. My life depends on them. And even if you don't live in a small town, this is true for you as well: your life depends on the high standards and kindness of the people who take care of you and your community, all of whom are someone's former students. It's a good reminder about what really matters in education.

I no longer teach in our town's public school, but I am pleased to say that it remains a wonderful place for children. Families may worry at times about a bear or moose crossing the playground, but they rarely worry that the adults in the school will not get to know their child well, believe in her potential for great things, push her to succeed, and value her as a whole person.

For the past 15 years I have had the privilege of working full-time for a non-profit organization, EL Education (formerly, Expeditionary Learning), that I have supported since its creation in 1993. I am fortunate to continually grow as an educator and person through my work, learning from remarkable people—teachers, leaders, and students in our partner schools, and colleagues on our staff. My collection of beautiful student work has grown every year, thanks to talented and generous students and teachers across the country and beyond. It is now the world's largest collection of high-quality student work, and lives online on a free website, *Models of Excellence*[1], curated by my colleagues at EL Education and Harvard Graduate School of Education.

I wrote this book at an inflection point for public education in America, and a great deal has changed since. No Child Left Behind, state standards, and high-stakes testing had just been instituted; public charter schools had just begun; the internet had just become a part of education. Yet many things have not changed at all. The mission of public education—to prepare students to be informed, capable, just, and compassionate citizens of our democracy—remains the same. Engaging our youth to do their best work and treat others with respect is no easier now than it ever was. We still deeply underestimate the capacity of our students and teachers, and focus on "fixing" individuals rather than building school cultures that bring

---

1. modelsofexcellence.ELeducation.org

out the best in all of us.

As a nation, we are still grasping for quick "solutions" to improving schools, when we know that there is no magic fix in education. Quality education comes from one place: a culture of quality that permeates a school. In Hollywood movies, success is almost always the product of one inspirational teacher who loves and pushes her students despite overwhelming odds. There are real-life teachers like that—I have been privileged to meet some. But hoping for individual heroic teachers is not an answer to improving education. While it may not make for an easy Hollywood story, our real work is still to build and maintain school cultures of high standards in all domains—in academics and arts, in critical thinking and creativity, in responsibility and respect, and in equity and social justice. That was not easy twenty-five years ago and it's just as difficult today. There is no shortcut around the relentless daily commitment to quality.

When this book was first published, many educators questioned if the school culture it described—which demanded much more of teachers and students, and trusted them with powerful responsibility and agency—was only possible in its unusual setting: a small, rural one-school district in New England. I have good news to share in that regard. Most of my work with EL Education for the past 15 years has been in urban settings, often in large districts, and often with students and educators of color—a very different setting from my small town. The quality of teaching and learning I have seen in many of the schools I have been privileged to work with has surpassed anything I describe in this essay. I believe it is possible anywhere.

I begin this essay describing a scientific study that my sixth-grade students led, in collaboration with a local college, to test the homes in our town for radon gas. Though the project is now twenty-five years old, the scientific report they created is still so important that I received a request this fall from the town Board of Health for a digital copy, as they could not locate the hard copy in Town Hall. My students took on adult-level responsibility in managing this project and were held to professional standards for their data and writing. People's lives were at stake. Quality standards were absolute. But is that story just another "teacher hero" story? Does it have any relevance to other schools in very different settings?

If you visit the *Models of Excellence* website, you will find hundreds of examples of schools across the country, many of them urban schools working with low-income students, who have prepared and empowered students to lead important and original research. Students ranging in age from kindergartners to high school seniors have tested water quality in their communities, mapped tree installations, interviewed local veterans, immigrants, civil rights activists, and scientists, and have created professional-quality books to honor their stories. They have created interpretative signs and field guides to local parks, waterfronts, city centers, and museums. They have created films, podcasts, PSAs, websites, and political campaigns to work for justice and environmental protection. And students in all of these schools, just as the rural students I describe in this essay, regularly present evidence of their work and their growth in public presentations of learning.

In the past fifteen years, I have spent very little time in our town's elementary school, but I have spent a good deal of time in the nearest city, Springfield, Massachusetts, at the Springfield Renaissance School. Renaissance is a public, district secondary school, founded as an EL Education School, that empowers its students and teachers to be leaders of their own learning, sharing their work regularly with each other and the community. Renaissance students engaged in original research in which they were trained by city engineers to conduct energy audits for city buildings. Their scientific and financial report resulted in the city investing over $150,000 to renovate city schools, all of which was made back in energy savings within two years, saving the city money and helping the environment. With a student population of about 700, primarily low-income students of color, and no selective admission process, Renaissance has remarkable results. 98% of students are graduating high school on time, and 100% of graduates for ten consecutive years have been admitted to college.

Why is this school so successful when so many urban high schools are struggling? It would be handy if we could point to a single reason—a structure, a strategy—and credit its success to that, something we might easily copy. The truth, as you already know, is that there is nothing simple about its success. Renaissance staff work their tails off every single day to cultivate and sustain a school culture where students and staff are physically and emotionally safe, where character is inseparable from academics, and where standards are high. It's remarkably hard work to maintain a culture of quality, but it's the most important work there is.

Ron Berger
Amherst, Massachusetts
February, 2019

Foreword

There is a common perception that today's schools are in crisis. People are grasping for solutions—longer days, new management structures, alternative assessments, and fresh curriculum, even a return to curriculum from the past. Though I support many of the initiatives being proposed, I think there is a real danger in assuming there is any quick fix or a single strategy that will 'save' schools.

THIS QUOTE from Ron Berger's essay *A Culture of Quality: A Reflection on Practice*, first published by the Annenberg Institute in 1996, is as true now, fifteen years later, as it was then—unfortunately for our schools and students. Our nation's public schools are entering another round of standards and assessment development that will compel a realignment of current school reform efforts. For this reason, Berger's reflections on improving the quality of practice in individual classrooms by creating a culture of quality in the entire school bears revisiting—especially for urban school communities serving students with serious challenges and undervalued assets.

In 2011, a decade of data arising from No Child Left Behind requirements has made it painfully clear that chronic failure and persistent achievement gaps between students advantaged and disadvantaged by income, language, and zip code are as serious as ever, if not worse. This has created a new sense of urgency and fueled a national conversation about school reform ripe with references about the need for immediate change through new standards and assessments, new evaluation and data systems, new technologies, and alternative sources of human talent.

While these largely technical approaches have potential to transform teaching and learning, Berger reminds us that this will fail if practitioners and policymakers ignore the need to change school cultures that foster isolation and distrust among adults (teachers, school administrators, parents) and students.

In an essay marked by its insight and humility, Berger reflects on his own classroom experience to demonstrate how the attainment of quality depends on creating cultural change that sets high academic standards for every single student as well as high expectations for more abstract qualities like kindness, integrity, and responsibility. He reminds us that "elements that have nothing to do with curriculum often have the most profound effect on the lives of children."

Above all, his essay is an eloquent reminder that sustainable school reforms must be engineered from the classroom out rather than solely from the top down. At the small school in Massachusetts described in this book, it is deep connections between teachers, between teachers and students, and between school and community that nourish excellence—not mandates from above. And in his new preface,

Berger shares the heartening news that the same approach has proven effective in urban schools. This resonates with our work at the Annenberg Institute, which has shown us that individual school reforms do not take place in isolation—they must be embedded in a school-wide, district-wide, and community-wide network of supports and mutual accountability. We call such a network a "smart educational system." A growing number of other education reformers today advocate similar approaches.

Building equitable and excellent systems of schools at scale takes time, investment, public will, and profound cross-sector collaboration. In a public discourse too often characterized by conflicting ideologies and extreme positions, this new edition of *A Culture of Quality* reminds us of those lessons.

Warren Simmons
Executive Director
Annenberg Institute for School Reform
July 2011

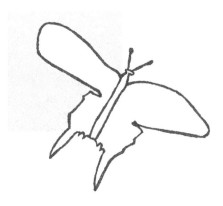

INTRODUCTION

An Opportunity Arises

ONE SATURDAY NIGHT in early December a year or so ago, I ran into a friend at an Italian restaurant. Though my friend is a college professor and I am an elementary school teacher, our teaching philosophies and strategies are so similar that we have often worked together. Our ideas for collaboration come so quickly and with such excitement that they inevitably ruin dinners for our families. While we should say a polite hello and agree to get back in touch, we inevitably end up asking a few questions that tumble into wild and intricate schemes for common projects.

This time, however, I was safe. My friend, John Reid, teaches geology and earth sciences at Hampshire College, and my sixth-grade students were immersed in an interdisciplinary study that entailed physical science but certainly not geology. My class was at the culmination of a study of deafness, sound, and hearing. They were becoming experts in the anatomy of the ear, the physics of sound. They studied the history of the Deaf, the political issues facing the Deaf, and had an ongoing relationship with members of the local Deaf community. They were becoming competent users of American Sign Language and worked with Deaf students in a bilingual school and in an oral school. I was tremendously pleased with how this study was going and was not about to deviate from it to start a new project.

Or so I thought.

I'd underestimated John's power to lure me into his passions. John has a unique approach to teaching. There are so many vital and exciting topics to research, he feels, that it just makes sense to get students immediately involved in running a real research project. Whether they're graduate students with advanced skills or freshmen with few skills makes no difference to him. They can learn skills as they work; and at the end of their semester or year, they'll have more than a grade or a test score—they'll have a published paper, or a set of data that is somehow valuable in the real world. They will understand real-life, adult science. It is no wonder that so many of the students who take John's introductory course, often with little prior interest, end up as scientists.

If it works with college freshmen, why not with sixth graders? That might sound a little crazy, but eight years ago my class had tested the water purity in the private wells of the homes in our town, and people took it very seriously. Not only was the school deluged with phone calls from families anxiously awaiting test results, but the local newspapers, town Board of Health, Conservation Commission, and even the town lawyer called for updates. (All of these callers had to speak to students, of course, as students were running all aspects of the project, including public disclosure and press.)

That project had been a perfect collaboration: elementary school students educated the town, managed the sample collection, and brought the samples to John Reid's laboratory. In the lab, college students taught the fifth and sixth graders how to run the analysis machines, and the elementary kids analyzed the samples, with the help of John and his students.

But this was all old news. The water study had been a great success, but that was a long time ago. My new students had their own all-consuming study, and they were brimming with pride in their work There was no way I would consider changing my entire focus.

"Ronnie!" John shouted across the restaurant. "I've got the perfect project—radon!"

Radon? Now I knew what radon was—a colorless, odorless, dangerous gas that infiltrates many homes and buildings—but it had no connection whatsoever to our current study of the Deaf, as I quickly explained to John. John, however, paid no attention to my futile efforts to preserve my curriculum. He hopped up from his chair, stroked his shaggy beard, and looked at me with that wild glint in his eye. Within seconds, he was on a roll and, before I could stop him, he had planned our collaboration for the entire upcoming month.

"So, first we turn your students into radon experts," he gasped, "and that will be easy because I can come in and do lectures and bring my students and the state radon specialist is a great guy and he has curriculum materials and I can teach your students some data analysis and graphing..." (I found it hard to fit in my words of protest) "...and then your students can educate the school and the community," he continued, "and put together packets with test canisters to distribute—of course with some extra canisters from a private test company to ensure our accuracy—then my students can set up the test equipment and..."

It was hopeless. He was suggesting a project that would provide a vital service to the town and its health, would save families money, would teach science and data analysis and an ethic of service to my students, and would provide a picture of town radon levels that was, in itself, a valuable scientific document, perhaps the first such document in the state. He had the equipment, the background, the resources. All I had to do was let go of my plans and say yes. We stood in the restaurant between tables, leaving our families shaking their heads as usual, and I knew there was no way I could say no.

SECTION ONE

The Radon Project

THE FOLLOWING MONDAY, I sat down with my principal and gave him my pitch; this study would entail postponing or eliminating much of a month's curriculum, so I had to be a good salesman. My students would learn fundamentals of data analysis, of professional quality experimental technique, and of scientific writing. They would be inter- viewing, surveying, teaching, writing letters, drafting tables and graphs, and putting together a serious report for the town. As it turned out, there was not much salesmanship needed—my principal was pleased and supportive from the start.

My students were disappointed to have to cut back on their Deaf studies for a month and made sure that the most vital aspects of the study continued without interruption. They were excited, however, when they learned of the responsibility that this project would confer upon them. Many of them had heard of the water study and realized that they were about to become part of a project with that kind of importance.

MOTIVATION

Radon is nothing to take lightly. It is the second leading cause of lung cancer in this country, after smoking. There is no way to tell if it is a problem in a home without testing, nor even to guess with any assurance that a home is low-risk. The chances were almost certain that we would discover dangerous levels in some homes in town. It is a treatable condition, but ridding a house of radon can run to several thousand dollars of expense and could seem overwhelming to families of low income.

The students soaked in the lectures and readings about radon and radioactive decay of elements with a passion not usually afforded to these subjects. There would be no test on the concepts. The stakes were much higher: the students would themselves be teachers of children and adults in town, and if they didn't understand this stuff perfectly, the consequences were obvious. Students knew that families could be nervous and even perhaps quite upset during the testing process and results. They themselves had to be calm, clear, and informed.

Learning from Past Experience

Everything went smoothly at first. But no project of this scale goes forward easily, and I was ever suspicious that serious problems lay just around the corner. Having encountered difficulties over the confidentiality of results during the earlier water study, I made sure we organized this aspect of the research carefully. During the water study, we were well into our data analysis before it really sank in for us how serious and immediate the repercussions could be for families: perceptions of safety and values of real estate could change overnight from our findings; families might find their homes declared off limits for friends of their children.

This time we planned ahead: all canisters and packets were number-coded and the codes kept in the school safe. Every family's privacy was ensured. We had long discussions about sensitivity in distribution of results and about providing help for families with problem houses. My students were on the phone with the town lawyer frequently during this initial period.

The radon canisters were accompanied by an informational packet written by students and a survey concerning the home being tested. The survey asked about features of the house that might correlate with radon levels. We intended to graph the results of this survey to see if the age of the house, the level of insulation, the type of foundation, or other features might bear a relationship to the level of radon. We also intended to plot results on a town map in order to search for geographic patterns in the radon levels.

During all of this work, John Reid was a guide and mentor to the class and to me. He and his Hampshire College students visited our class for lessons, and I stopped by his lab with questions. Things went forward without a flaw. The sixth graders gave presentations and lessons to younger students in our school; packets were distributed and collected from families; canisters were tested; individual house results were confidentially returned. This was really working! All that remained was to sort through all of the data and prepare a report. True, this was the bulk of the work involved in the project, but I wasn't worried.

What could go wrong now?

Learning on the Job

As we were closing up school for the winter holiday break, with all our data collected and ready to analyze, John casually mentioned to me that he was leaving for Death Valley for a research project with a group of students. He wouldn't be back for a month. He held up a disk with all the results of our work-—over five thousand pieces of data—and said, "Ronnie, you know how to use a database program, don't you? You just have to teach your students, and you'll have a blast with this data! Microsoft Excel is such a fun program. They'll love it! Well, I gotta run..."

I grabbed him before he could leave. "John," I pleaded, "you can't just leave at this point! I've never used Microsoft Excel. I've done almost no work with database and spreadsheet programs. I'll have no idea what I'm doing!"

He beamed in his jovial way. "You'll love it! It's a great program. You have a Macintosh at home, right? And one in your classroom, right? You'll have a blast. It's pretty much self-explanatory."

Kids of today seem to be hard-wired for swift acquisition of computer skills. I am an older-generation model, and there is no built-in chip in my brain that makes learning new software a snap. My entire holiday vacation was spent camped at my computer, teaching myself how to use Excel. I began with one of those "Excel for Idiots" books. It was right at my level. After three or four days, I graduated to a regular Excel handbook, and at the end of a week, I ventured into an enormous volume titled Excel in Business. I was, literally, at my computer every night until midnight and beyond. The town was anxiously awaiting results, and everything depended on my competence (or lack thereof) with this confusing software. I had stomachaches.

Back in the classroom after vacation, things began to look up. Luckily, my students were much quicker at mastering Excel than I. Though we only had one computer in the classroom, it was in use every minute of the day in January. I did group and individual instruction, but most of the teaching was student to student, once one of them was up to speed. Even my most academically challenged students worked at the computer with a partner and organized data accurately.

With all the hype about new technology, I occasionally wonder about the real value of computers in a classroom. This was not one of those times. The sorting and tabulation of data, the transformation of data using equations, and the creation of tables and graphs—all operations which my students were doing in minutes—would take days or even weeks of work with a pocket calculator, graph paper, and a patient worker. Students were split into teams of two or three to attack particular survey questions or geographical grid sectors. Each team had somewhere between five hundred and a thousand items of data to organize and make sense of; each had the responsibility for preparing charts, graphs, and a written explanation of their findings for the report.

Focused Work

For the next three weeks, the room had the feel of a newspaper office just before publication. Sheets of paper were strewn everywhere; some contained word-processed scientific explanations of findings being critiqued and reworked by teams of students. Most contained columns of numbers, highlighted in different colors, with scribbles in the margins. Students checked results on calculators and negotiated for computer time. Nothing was included in the report until it had been checked, critiqued, and redrafted, and until the whole class approved.

The final report was entirely student-made, down to the paste- up, the xeroxing, the collating, and the stapling. But while it was researched and written by eleven-year-olds, it was taken very seriously by the adult world. Every town governance committee received a copy, and many individuals on the committees requested copies of their own. Copies went to local press, local health officials, and schools. Some readers suggested that we submit our report for publication to a scientific journal.

When it became clear that this was the first-known comprehensive radon picture of any town in the state, requests for copies mounted. We went into a second and third printing as other towns and schools, as well as county, state, and even federal radon scientists, wanted copies. Students answered each request individually, word- processing a personal response and enclosing additional background information. Just when I thought we could return to normal life, the classroom had turned into a not-for-profit business, our windowsills stacked with reports and mailing envelopes.

As I write this account of the project, more than a year has passed since the report's first publication. The researchers/authors have left my school and are now students in a regional junior high school in another town, but they come back often to visit. When they do, I update them about the ongoing requests for copies of the report and we smile with pride.

ANALYZING OUR SUCCESS

After the whirlwind of publishing our first edition, I had time to breathe and reflect. One night, as I was leaning against the cool concrete wall in my school's gym, hot and sweaty after a basketball game, I began describing the past month to a teammate. I was so proud of my students, so pleased at how things had come together. He responded with a question: "Why do you think this project turned out so well?" It was a simple question, but I found I had no simple answer. The more I tried to explain, the more complexities and surprises I turned up.

It was a good curriculum idea.

It was a good idea, to be sure. But in this "age

of curriculum," when textbook companies and school boards attempt to develop and mandate "teacher-proof" curriculum, curriculum so detailed that a robot could "deliver" it, this study was just the opposite. It was brand new curriculum, built from scratch, without clear models or deadlines or mandated lessons. The very nature of the study necessitated flexible work times, interdisciplinary understanding, and creative, responsible management of time and effort by the students as well as the teacher. In short, just about everything could have gone wrong in this project. The classroom could have been chaos, the research a disaster. The curriculum idea in and of itself did not guarantee any success.

There was some inspired teaching.

This was true, but very little of it was what we usually think of as teaching—the stand-at-the-blackboard-and-dazzle teaching that is celebrated in books and movies. John Reid did a little of this: he gave two or three lectures that were impassioned, clear, humorous, and brilliantly metaphorical. But most of the teaching was something very different. My time was spent as an organizer and co-researcher— setting up the physical classroom and the work groups, scheduling critique and discussion sessions, finding examples of similar research to model, troubleshooting. My teaching centered on knowing each individual student well enough to understand when and how they would need support and with whom to partner them. My approach was predicated on a fundamental trust that students would take all of this seriously and do their absolutely best work. Without this precondition of student disposition, the teaching would not have succeeded.

These were gifted kids.

All of my students are gifted in different ways. In terms of traditional labels, however, this was not a "gifted and talented" class. It was a regular sixth-grade class in a regular public school. The town in which the school is situated is a rural one with working-class and middle- class families. The school has a fully inclusionary special education program, so that children of different needs are not separated from the classroom or removed from the classroom for their work. In this particular classroom, one-third of the students were on educational plans for academic needs, and these students did as much of the project as anyone else.

So why was this study so successful?

THE KEY TO OUR SUCCESS: SCHOOL CULTURE

It was successful because it was introduced into a school culture into which it fit perfectly—a culture of quality. The students with whom I worked had been prepared for years (some for as many as seven years, beginning in preschool) to take on the responsibility of mature, self- directed work and to do that work to extremely high standards. There was a history in this school of students taking on significant original projects and original research. Students were accustomed to presenting their work to the world beyond their classrooms. To the younger students in the school, to the teachers in the school, and to the community, it made perfect sense to have sixth graders acting as educators and researchers on an adult-level project. The school and community took the project seriously and supported it at all junctures.

Wherever I go, I describe my teaching situation as privileged. It is not privileged in the traditional sense of the word. As I said, I teach in a regular public school in a small, rural town. Neither the town nor the school has much money; our per-pupil spending is near the bottom in the state; our salaries wouldn't make anyone jealous. The privilege for me lies in being part of a school with a school culture of quality. Our staff is small, and we have great respect for each other's teaching. Though we agree unanimously on little during staff meetings, we share a common vision for the school, one marked by an expectation of quality, a pride in quality, and a striving for quality. The administration trusts the staff to work together toward this vision, to build the school's curriculum, and to make important decisions, such as hiring and use of school funds. We are a public school that does not use textbooks and worksheets or give grades (and has not for twenty years); yet the town, a fairly conservative rural community, supports the school and celebrates its nontraditional approach. The townspeople do not support the school because the techniques it uses are now considered "innovative" or "current." They support the school because their kids succeed: they are strong readers, writers, and users of math; they are responsible, courteous, and motivated; they do well in life.

Our school is far from perfect. Our staff meetings are often consumed with exasperation as we discuss weak points, whether it be the level of spelling at a certain grade, the level of politeness shown at recess, or the social adjustment of a single, troubled child. A strong culture takes constant vigilance, revision, and patience. The pride and responsibility in children, the morale and vision of staff, need continual reaffirmation. We are often exhausted. Still, many of us have been together for fifteen or twenty years without "burning out." Supporting a culture of quality is tiring, but at the same time inspiring and nourishing.

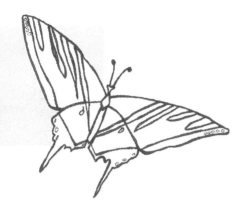

SECTION TWO

What Is a Culture of Quality?

THERE IS A COMMON PERCEPTION that today's schools are in crisis. People are grasping for solutions—longer days, new management structures, alternative assessments, fresh curriculum, even a return to curriculum from the past. Though I support many of the initiatives being proposed, I think there is a real danger in assuming there is any quick fix or single strategy that will "save" schools.

The quality of a school lies in its culture. Particular aspects of the school—budget, curriculum, teaching roles, decision making, assessment, physical layout—are elements of this culture but do not in themselves define it. The only way to understand a school culture is to understand what students experience in being part of it. Not just the motivated, mainstream students, but also the students who look or feel different. How safe do students feel, physically and emotion- ally? What kind of pride and intensity is encouraged for work? What values, what sense of courtesy and responsibility are modeled? A school culture of quality connotes a culture of high standards for all students in all domains: standards for academic achievement, arts, physical fitness, critical thinking, and creativity, but also standards for kindness, integrity, industriousness, and responsibility. Some schools renowned for high test scores sustain a culture where students carry an air of entitlement and are disrespectful or cruel to each other, where students who don't "fit," due to race, class, or physical differences, are alienated and mistreated.

I would like to offer here a vision of a positive school culture based on a real-life model—this is the vision that I and my colleagues hold for the school in which we teach. The premises and strategies underlying the culture are not our invention. Although I try to describe them in practice here, I take no credit for them and I acknowledge that they derive from many sources. Because I am a teacher, the illustrations that follow are often from my own classroom, but they reflect the wider school culture that sustains them.

If what follows runs counter to the ideas of today's educators and reformers, whether "progressive" or "traditional," it is because I feel that people in general are not looking deeply enough at schools and children.

WHAT GOES ON IN THE HALLWAYS IS AS IMPORTANT AS WHAT GOES ON IN THE CLASSROOM

To understand how a school culture shapes the attitudes of children, one must understand that elements having nothing to do with curriculum often have the most profound effect on the lives of children. The aspects of a school that most clearly engrave the school experience on children are often in the "other stuff" category: the physical appearance of the school building, outside and in; the manner in which school property and personal property are respected and cared for in the school; the levels of physical safety and emotional safety that children and adults in the building feel; the way routines of arrival, class transitions, lunch times, and dismissal are handled; the ways authority is exercised; the tone of courtesy, kindness, and acceptance in peer culture; the ways in which student achievements are shared within the school community and outside of it; the aspects of the school that define it in the larger community. These things are every bit as important as curriculum.

"Oh, yeah, those things," people may say. "Well, of course, those are important; those go without thinking." The problem is, those things don't go well without thinking, and they don't go well in many of the schools in this country. To keep a school clean and in good repair, filled with displays of beautiful student work, to maintain an environment where students feel safe from physical danger, exclusion, or ridicule, where people are polite and patient and helpful, and where all the students have forums in which they can succeed and take pride in their work—this is no easy job. It requires a school culture that takes real time in the day— time away from curriculum, time "off task"—to sustain such a culture.

My sixth-grade students are assistants to the school cooks in the cafeteria and to the custodian in the lunch room. They set up the library for assemblies and the gym for events. When the school secretary is absent, they run the office. They are responsible for cleaning and caring for the classroom, and caring for classroom animals. They each have kindergarten advisees whom they tutor and help in school and on the bus. If there is a problem on the playground or in the hallways with my students not treating others kindly, they know that nothing in the curriculum is going to take precedence over a group discussion and consequences regarding that behavior. None of this is curriculum, as we usually define the term.

Part of maintaining a culture of quality is taking the time as a school staff to build and sustain structures, traditions, and rituals to make sure these realms of school are positive. Most schools have "school codes" that remind students to "treat others well." If, how- ever, these same schools ignore exclusion and mean behavior in the lunchroom and hallways or tolerate disrespect for student belongings or feelings in the school yard, the code means little. Schools that strictly enforce and celebrate polite and kind behavior, that regularly use staff meetings to discuss behavioral issues, that actively use community meetings, peer mediation, peer tutoring, mentor programs, community service work, and community exhibitions of excellence, must take a lot of time planning things that aren't purely curricular. It is time well spent, because quality in one area supports quality throughout the system.

There are no short cuts to building and maintaining a school community of courtesy and kindness, of integrity and responsibility. Some families, in exasperation, remove their children from public schools and place them in parochial or military schools, looking for a strict environment. I think strictness is essential, and I credit many of these schools with taking issues of character and physical environment seriously. But strict rules alone are not the answer: they maintain order but do not guarantee that children will treat each other well or feel good about themselves. Prisons have plenty of strict rules. What is necessary is a school community that not only demands the best of its students in terms of character but that models that character through school tone, routines, and practices.

In the end, I would be surprised if anyone really thinks that these things are less important than curriculum. I would be surprised, too, if anyone who really took the time to think about these issues could conclude that they could be attended to with little effort, in the margins of the school day, rather than as a primary and explicit priority and commitment of time, all day, every day.

LESS CAN BE BETTER

More hours, more days, more assignments, more homework—there is an obsession with quantity these days. I believe the obsession should be with quality instead. I have no problem with sweat, hard work, and challenge; I relish it and demand it. But I am concerned with the quality of what such hard work produces.

Schools can sometimes take on the feel of a production shop, students cranking out an endless flow of final products without much personal investment or care. The emphasis is on keeping up with production, on not falling behind in class work or homework, rather than on producing something of lasting value. As in a fast-food restaurant, the products are neither creative nor memorable. Teachers create and perpetuate this situation, even though they grow tired of repetitive, trivial assignments and dread correcting piles of such work.

Turning in final draft work every day, often many times in one day, forces even the most ambitious of students to compromise standards continually, simply to keep up the pace. Internalized high standards are no antidote to a system that demands final draft work at this rate. If an adult writer, scientist, historian, or artist were asked to turn in a stack of finished pieces of work every day, how much care could he or she put into each? The same phenomenon occurs with "getting through" textbooks. Textbooks rule curriculum and time; in-depth critical discussion, thought, and original research must be cut short, or cut altogether, because there are always more pages, more exercises to get through, and the year is only so long.

One alternative is a project-centered approach, in which students still work hard every day, but each day's work is a small but meaningful part of a long-range, significant project. Daily work entails the creation or revision of early drafts of a piece or the continued research of a topic or the management of an experiment or the perfection of one component of a large piece of work. Final drafts or presentations of completed projects are no longer trivial events occurring every day but special events, moments of individual and class pride and celebration.

This longer process allows time for students to produce work of real personal value and of substantial depth and quality. It allows time for multiple drafts, rehearsals, or experimental trials. It allows time for serious critique of unfinished work—teacher critique, peer critique, and self-critique. It allows the teacher and the class community to set rigorous standards for final drafts and presentations and requires that they be met.

Qualities of a Good Project

There is no one good model for such projects. I've seen a range of successful ideas and structures in different schools, from first graders publishing novels for their school library to fourth graders creating field guides to local ponds to eighth graders preparing development plans for vacant lots based on surveys of neighborhood residents. Across the range, though, there are common features to the successful projects I've seen. All allow, indeed require, students to be creative, to make decisions, and to take real responsibility for their own work. All include a substantial focus on learning new academic and artistic skills and perfecting those skills in practice. All use the project as a framework in which skills are acquired and polished. And, importantly, all provide a forum for sharing finished work with a wider audience.

These projects are different from the project model that I call the "science-fair" model. When I was a student in elementary school, the only substantial projects we worked on were science projects. The structure was as follows: The teacher would say to the class, "Next month is our science fair. I'd like you all to submit a project. They are due May ninth. Good luck." These projects were completed entirely out of school, which meant that students who came from privileged homes (and I use privilege not just in terms of wealth but in terms of emotional and organizational stability) had a tremendous advantage over students who did not. In fact, we students could never tell how much of the work of others was done by parents (and I'm not sure the teachers could either).

These science-fair projects were not a culmination of classroom learning, but topics chosen at random, pursued without critical assistance from peers or teachers. We were not taught the importance of breaking down the project into manageable steps nor were we required to do so; we were not even taught time management. Some kids always started early, but I was one of the last-minute kids and I made life miserable for my family the night before due date. (People say that you learn from the consequences of your mistakes, but I didn't seem to: I went through same painful panic every year.) Moreover, we were not taught standards for assessing these projects. We couldn't aim for quality because we had no real sense of what quality was.

On the day of the fair, some students brought in impressive- looking work, some students (I among them) brought in last-minute work. Many students brought in awful work or no work at all; for them, the project was a total failure. Then, ribbons magically appeared on some projects, but it was never the ones we thought should win. Not understanding the criteria for judging nor having any back- ground in the subjects explored by others, we were always more taken with the visually impressive posters than the experiments that represented good science.

Quality Entails Universal Success

In contrast, the project model I propose is predicated on every single student succeeding. And this doesn't mean every student finishing, but rather every student finishing something that represents the best of his or her talents. This model does not preclude work at home, but it uses the school as the hub of creation, as a project workshop. The overall quality of work to emerge from this workshop, not just individual quality, is a vital and explicit concern. If any student is failing to succeed, if any student is producing work without effort or care, it is a problem for the whole workshop.

The project must therefore be structured to make it impossible for individuals to fail or fall far behind. Through continual conferences, critique sessions, and peer and teacher support, student progress is sustained and assessed at all points during the creation process.

Projects are planned with distinct check points through which each student passes on the road to completion, with explicit methods and procedures that must be followed at each stage. The resulting display of completed projects from such a workshop, such a class, is characterized by universal success and whole-class pride.

Universal success does not mean uniformity. Although the structure that braces and guides student progress is common to every project, each student's project is unique. The structure provides a frame for common learning and critique, as well as for appraisal of progress, but it also leaves room for significant creative expression and direction by individual students. If every student in a classroom prepares a guidebook to a different local building, the steps and skills involved may be somewhat prescribed—conducting interviews, researching local history, consulting city records, trying to obtain blueprints, doing sketches, taking photographs, preparing diagrams, writing and proofreading drafts of text, preparing illustrations, composing book layout, learning book binding. Within this frame, however, individual students have substantial latitude for artistic choices—the selection of building, the decision of whom to interview, the use of research and interviews, the nature of text and illustrations, the balance of text and illustrations, the use of photographs or diagrams, the tone of presentation, the layout of the finished book.

As much as possible, these projects should represent "real work," work that is original and offers something of value to a wider community. When my students interviewed senior citizens to prepare biographies of their lives, they were doing something much more than a classroom exercise. They were building relationships and working to provide an artifact that might be treasured by that senior and his or her family for the rest of their lives. The reason for high standards of research, organization, written language, and visual presentation in these biographies was clear to the students: this was real, important work. There was a clear reason for the students to learn twentieth-century history, interview techniques, shorthand, tape transcription, photography, illustration, research skills. And they applied what they learned immediately.

Such projects represent more than just a mastery of skills; they demonstrate an internalized dedication and competence in planning and crafting high-quality work. Once a student leaves school, she is judged for the rest of her life on her ability to produce such work, not on her ability to take tests or answer questions at the end of a chapter. To structure learning around the creation of quality work, rather than around the ability to memorize facts, seems not only sensible but vital in preparing students for life.

THE MOST IMPORTANT ASSESSMENT IN SCHOOLS IS DONE BY STUDENTS, NOT TEACHERS

When the word assessment is used, the first thing that comes to mind for most people is testing. Schools in this country administer annually over a hundred million mandated tests at a cost of over a billion dollars. American students are tested far more than the students of other countries, and to what end? Rather than focusing on creating environments that breed healthy learners, our schools treat all students as sick patients, taking their temperatures constantly and even publishing them in the local paper.

I think assessment has been confused with ranking. I will admit that it is difficult to rank students without numerical results of tests or performance assessments, and I will admit that there are times when it may be important to rank students. But I believe these times are rare. I use tests in my classroom occasionally, though not to rank. I teach test-taking as a life skill: because the academic world, unlike the real world, judges personal merit so much by test-taking ability, it would be a terrible disservice not to help my students learn to take tests effectively.

But in our school, assessment means much more than testing. Every time a student produces a piece of work in our school, he or she assesses it while it is in process, and assesses it again before turning it in. If it is to be redrafted, it has been assessed yet again when re-turned with comments, and later the new draft is assessed for quality. The quality of what is produced depends upon the assessment skills the individual student has developed. If schools feel a need to obsess about assessment, it is this level of assessment on which the obsession should dwell—this is the level of assessment that determines quality.

Every student carries around with him or her a picture of acceptable standards, a notion of what his or her work should look like before it is handed in or before it is a finished piece. This picture is a vision of how accurate, neat, thorough, thoughtful, original, and elegant a piece of work should be. This should be a vital concern of every school: What is the picture of quality in the heads of our students? Not our "gifted" students or our "motivated" students, but what is it in all our students? What is it in a student chosen at random in the hallway? And, most important, how can we get into the heads of our students and sharpen that picture as needed?

The Language of Critique

A vision of quality can be learned, and it can continually develop. If schools can step off the treadmill of work production and decide to focus on fewer pieces of work, refining these thoughtfully, there are many strategies they can adopt to this end. One is to set a realistic time frame for high-quality, finished work, setting out in advance for students the idea that they are embarking on a serious commitment to produce something powerful, and that time and multiple drafts will be required.

Self-assessment is only as strong as the vocabulary and conceptual depth of the student doing the assessment. Teachers must model assessment by taking exemplary pieces of work and flawed pieces of work and dissecting them with students, building the vocabulary of critique in the process. These examples can be taken from well-known resources; but it is often more helpful to use actual work of current or past students, as long as the feelings of students are protected. For most projects, I produce a sample piece of work that is very strong in many ways, flawed in others, and spend a great deal of time pulling it apart with students and building vocabulary and vision as we do so. With the permission of students, I often save particularly strong examples of student projects from past years and keep them in a portfolio at school. I use these samples to set a high base level of expectation for the current class (which they try to exceed) when I introduce a project. My students are so enamored of this portfolio that they constantly finger through it, admire it, ask questions about it, and critique the work within it.

We have regular critique sessions in my classroom. The work critiqued may be writing, drafting, experimental design, even a mathematical solution. Sometimes the work of every child is pinned up for review and feedback. Sometimes only a single piece of work is the critique focus, and it is done in real depth. In either case, we have a strict set of rules that governs critique etiquette. The rules exist to establish an environment safe from ridicule or sarcasm but equally to prevent wasting time on vague compliments. One particular rule is that statements such as "I like it" or "It's good" are not allowed: if the statements are not specific enough to assist the creator of the work or to enlighten the critique audience, we don't want to hear them. Critique is like surgery, cutting into a piece to find out what is working and what is not. The vocabulary of the domain is the kit of surgical tools. Using only words like "I like it" or "I don't like it" is like trying to do surgery with a butter knife.

The vocabulary of our critique sessions is basically the working vocabulary of practitioners in that field. For this reason, we like to have "experts," professionals or crafts people in a field, visit the school and teach us this vocabulary. To highlight an unusual example: One year, we hosted a nationally ranked collegiate women's soccer team. When my students began to model the language of the soccer players and the strategies they defined, both the style of play in the students' games and the level of their post-game analysis changed dramatically. They now had precise terms to describe particular passes, defenses, shots, movements, and they reveled in this new vocabulary on the field, shouting directions and ideas during games, even seeing options that wouldn't have occurred to them before, and playing quite differently.

There is never enough time to critique the work of every child in a group setting or even in individual teacher conferences. For this reason, group critiques, formal peer critiques, and formal teacher conferences merely build the skills and set the tone for the most significant critique—informal peer critique that is ubiquitous. I have no desks in my classroom; students work in small groups at tables. Whenever it is not a silent work time, the room is filled with students asking each other for suggestions, assistance, editing. Students wander around the room and offer critique and encouragement to each other continually.

The Role of Portfolios

The culture of critique in my classroom changed dramatically when I began to use portfolios. Although I had always saved student work for parent conferences, I hadn't realized the power of having comprehensive portfolios in supporting student reflection, investment, and pride. I learned that the key to portfolios wasn't in saving work; it was in using the work that was saved. My students these days have portfolios that weigh about eight pounds. (I know this because when- ever I borrow a few to share with teachers in another school, my arms are sore before I get there!) We use these fat collections of work constantly. Students are required to tune up portfolios regularly, to do regular portfolio searches for work that exhibits certain criteria, and to present parts or all of their portfolios regularly to a range of critical eyes—students, parents, teachers, community members.

When students present their portfolios to parents, it is a formal presentation and requires that parents fill out and return a reflection form to me, noting their reactions, thoughts, and concerns. At the end of each year, students prepare—with much discussion, critique, and rehearsal—a formal portfolio presentation for a panel, highlighting their accomplishments and profiling their strengths and weaknesses as learners. The panel consists of teachers from the junior high they will be entering, community members, and outside educators. Each presentation is videotaped by a student camera operator.

When I sat down to write out report cards this year, which in my school have narrative assessments rather than grades, I brought home four boxes of portfolios. I don't know how I ever did these progress reports without the portfolios to guide me. I get to know my students well, and five years ago I simply trusted my memory, my conference notes, and my account book of work turned in. Now I sit down with the collected work of each student, revisiting the small victories and leaps of understanding, recollecting the nagging problems in accuracy in a particular domain. I read the many self-evaluations my students write, evaluations of particular projects and holistic evaluations of strengths and weaknesses in life, and I weigh my judgment against their own.

The written descriptions I now send home to parents in report cards are stronger than those of past years in myriad ways. I can present a full and balanced picture, citing specific examples of work to celebrate strengths or key moments of growth and can give specific examples of areas needing growth, even quoting from a student's own reflection to make this clear. "Your son mentions in his self- evaluation that he feels he is 'kind of rude sometimes,... not in regular class but in music and in the lunchroom and stuff.' I think he is accurate here, and it's something we need to work on."

You will understand most clearly why I have become a portfolio advocate if you pay a visit to my school. A pair of students will give you what we call a curriculum tour of the building and end up in the classroom. There they will look at you with great expectation and pride and ask, "Would you be interested in seeing our portfolios?" And if you agree, they will smile and ask if you have an hour or two free to sit with them!

PEER PRESSURE SHOULD BE DIRECTED, NOT DISCOURAGED

All of my life I was told to avoid peer pressure. Peer pressure meant kids trying to talk you into smoking in the bathroom or ganging up to tease someone; always it meant being coerced into violating one's inner ethical wisdom and responsible nature. A few years ago it became clear to me, however, that our school is successful to a great extent because of peer pressure. Peer pressure can be a force for right as well as wrong. It is one of the strongest forces that govern the actions and attitudes of students at all ages, and it will be there whether schools and parents want it to be or not. It makes sense to me that schools recognize this power and actively shape it and direct it as a force for positive development.

When Quality Is Cool

Imagine a school in which to be cool, to fit in and be regarded as popular, you have to do quality work and treat others well. How do you build such an environment? If the school itself sanctions exclusion and hierarchy by supporting only the academic "stars" with awards, opportunities, exhibitions, and privileges, then quality work is regarded as the exception, not the norm. If the work of every child is going to be shared in an exhibition or presentation, and the merit of the school as a whole or the classroom as a whole will be judged by the overall quality of the entire exhibition, there is a reason for students to work together and push each other. It would be letting the class down, or letting the school down, to do less than quality work or to behave in a less than exemplary manner. Peer pressure would compel students to do a good job.

This dynamic, which may at first seem unlikely, is actually not hard to picture in some contexts. If a class were painting a mural on the wall of a city building, the work of every child would reflect on the class as a whole. It is easy to envision students being very concerned with high standards for each other's work. If a class is putting on a play or is engaged in a sporting event with another group, any student who does not know his or her lines or does not know how to play his or her position hurts the entire group. Students may need guidance in making their critique of others sensitive and constructive, but the pressure to do a good job will be unquestionable. This same pressure exists in my classroom as we build for a presentation of work—which, to varying degrees, we are always doing.

Pressure Has Its Rewards

A few years ago, I received a new student in the middle of the fall. This student was a seriously troubled young man, and his experiences had left him unwilling to trust adults, myself included. He had no reason even to assume I would be in his life very long, so investing me with authority and trust made no sense to him. I believe he would have had little success in my class if the peer culture had not shaped his development. He wanted to fit into the group, to be popular with the girls in the classroom, with the guys on the playground, and he found to his surprise that such acceptance required putting real effort into his work and behavior.

On one of his first days at the school, he saw a girl on the playground with a physical disability and began to mimic her. At his old school, this might have brought him some laughs and some positive attention from some of the boys. At our school, he found himself surrounded by a group of angry students. I had to speak sternly to the group and remind them that they shouldn't threaten someone, even to protect a person's feelings. In my heart, however, I found it difficult to be too angry with them. In fact, they were teaching the culture of their school, and the boy learned the lesson. That was the last time he tried something like that. To fit in in this school culture meant treating others well.

The first time he dashed off a piece of work, a student sitting next to him asked, "You're not going to turn that in, are you?" To which he responded, "Yeah! What does it matter to you?" Difficult words and disciplinary issues were often the result of my efforts to tune up his manner, but he did come to see that the other students regarded him as strange for his careless work and attitude. And on those occasions when he experimented with putting more time and care into something, he got very positive critique and encouragement from classmates, attention which he welcomed. Over the course of a few months, he began to produce his first work that, in his words, "was worth something." He said, "You know, I don't think I ever did something in school that I really cared about. This character file book is pretty cool. I can't believe I did this."

My sixth-grade students walk through a school library filled with novels written by first graders and fifth graders, maps of local ponds and amphibian field guides drafted by third and fourth graders, models of futuristic homes built by second graders. This is their school's heritage—impressive, meaningful projects—and as the oldest kids in the school, they feel compelled to show that their work is among the most striking and sophisticated. This is pressure, and it is positive pressure. Conversely, first graders look at the blueprints of homes designed by my students, drawn to scale with professional drafting equipment, and they wonder if they will be ready someday for that level of work. This too is pressure, also positive. In the peer culture of our school, to be cool means to contribute to this heritage of elegant and powerful work.

ART IS FUNDAMENTAL

It is possible to attend an educational conference on high standards in learning and never hear art mentioned. During times of crisis or crunch, art is the first subject schools discard. But, in the teaching approach I espouse, art is at the core of standards. It is not decoration but rather the primary context for work.

To understand what I mean requires a shift both in the adult conception of art as something for museums and concert halls and in the student conception of art as something that happens between 1:45 and 2:30 on Thursday afternoons (barring budget cuts). It means seeing art as inextricably a part of all that we produce and share, which is how many kindergartners naturally view it.

All student project work in our school is shared with others through some expressive medium. It may be expository writing, fiction, or poetry; drama, dance, or music; illustrations, diagrams, models, maps, photographs, or video; formal presentations or lessons; or, most commonly, some combination of these media. Moreover, every classroom project is viewed through aesthetic eyes, and viewers and producers both strive for aesthetic mastery.

An unspoken commandment in this classroom is that if you're going to share a final draft, a final presentation of a project, you do it well. You make it impressive, exciting, memorable. If it's a project in history or science, you not only research it with rigor, you also try to share it in a persuasive, elegant, and compelling manner. If it's a presentation, make it powerful! Use drama, music, slides, graphics, illustrations; refine and rehearse it. If it's a written project, include maps and diagrams, make a provocative cover, lay it out clearly and instructively; make it look good! All of these concerns, and the skills involved in addressing them, are part of this concept of art.

Setting Standards

I feel that standards for artistic expression must be central and passionate, not pushed aside. This doesn't mean adopting a traditional perspective of Western art, where the work of "masters" defines all standards. It does mean that art is a world of skills and knowledge, just like sports; and to learn to practice art well, one must look for and celebrate mastery in others.

It is not enough to ask students to make their work aesthetically powerful; they also must learn to understand and control aesthetic media. For this reason, a great deal of time in our school is spent learning and practicing artistic skills. When students are engaged in scientific projects, they learn drafting skills to create impressive charts and diagrams. When they are documenting a family history, they learn and perfect skills of ethnographic narrative in writing, of clarity and sensitivity in interviewing, and sometimes skills in photography or illustration. Some art lessons are planned outside the context of specific projects, because they are foundational and can empower students to approach projects with more sophistication. Occasional projects, such as plays, murals, or musical performances, are connected to themes of study but are also an opportunity to gain knowledge and mastery in a particular artistic domain.

Concepts of art, and artistic forms of learning and knowing, are treated with the same respect as all other disciplines of learning. Artistic aspects of project work are showered with time, attention, and quality materials. The use and care of quality materials—the kind that adult professionals use—contribute much to what might be called an elite sense of classroom standards. I encourage parents to use holiday and birthday gifts as opportunities to provide art supplies for their children. Using school funds, student-raised funds, and personal funds, I try to keep the classroom stocked so that no student is denied access to good materials.

Is This Really Art?

What constitutes "real art"? If illustration is regarded as an unimportant decoration for a report, if a fictional historical journal is judged simply for its historic content and not its aesthetic power, then I'm not sure. But that is not the case in our classrooms. The aesthetic components of work are given as much attention and critical guidance as any part of content.

Let me give a specific example: A few years back, several students of mine made a presentation to the whole school explaining the geological formation of the valley in which the school is situated. The content of their lesson was carefully prepared, critiqued by the class, and revised. Much time, however, was spent on the quality of their delivery. The information they needed to share wasn't difficult to gather, but the question of how to make that information clear and exciting to students as young as kindergartners was a different story. My students spent many days preparing carefully drafted and lettered charts and maps on large posterboard, getting critical feed- back from individual students and the class as a whole. The quality of illustration, the choice of lettering, the layout and composition, were discussed in the type of detail one might expect in the art department of an advertising firm. Their vocal presentation, even their physical movements during the presentation, were rehearsed and critiqued in front of the class. The result was remarkably different from the common experience of students nervously reading a report in front of a group. The difference, I think, was art.

The idea that the line between what is art

and what is not art should be hard to draw is not as strange as it first sounds. In the Japanese culture, for example, almost everything is viewed aesthetically. The way food is arranged on a plate, the way cleaning is done in a home, the way apologies are given to a friend—even the manner in which one dies may be viewed in aesthetic terms. Elegant samurai deaths were often planned far in advance and critiqued aesthetically for generations afterward. A Japanese friend of mine, preparing her résumé to send to prospective employers, told me that she drafted two copies: one typewritten, for American employers, and one done by hand in careful calligraphy, for Japanese employers. "They would never accept a typed version," she explained. "They judge my character by my calligraphy."

The concept that even the most mundane events and products may be crafted and executed with aesthetic care describes precisely my goal in the classroom. Rough drafts can be messy and confused; that's their purpose. But final drafts should be impressive, even on the smallest level. I know things are succeeding in this regard when math papers are turned in with elegant layouts and lettering, and when I find student notes on the floor done in calligraphy.

This concept of art cultivates a school and classroom culture where there are high standards for just about everything. There's no escaping them. Students even debate aesthetic arrangements for our giant turtle tank and stay in at recess to rearrange it.

DETAILS ARE IMPORTANT

For years, I have read that teaching and learning should be process-centered, not product-centered. Or perhaps person-centered—anything other than product-centered. For some time, I carried with guilt my passion for the beautiful artifacts my students created: they were only products; I shouldn't be so attached to them. But eventually I emerged from that educational closet to declare my love for the physical products that are the result of our studies. These products— books, maps, blueprints, models, sculptures, scientific reports, paintings, product designs—are treated with almost religious significance in my classroom. The tools we use to create them are treated with utmost respect and are generally professional quality rather than junior versions of tools ordered from a school supply firm. If all of our architectural templates are not returned in perfect condition, there is a price to pay.

An Obsession with Detail

We are obsessive about detail in my classroom and proud of it. If that means we are small-minded, so be it. To create beautiful fiction with- out concern for spelling and grammar makes a lot of sense to me. When that fictional piece reaches final draft, however, and is bound as a book and put on display for the community, spelling and gram- mar make a big difference, and obsessing about it is crucial. When students show me a technical diagram they've drawn that has graphic balance and artistic flair but is inaccurate in some of its technical detail, I don't accept it on effort. It goes back for another draft. Perhaps it can be traced (we built a light-table in my room to make tracing easy and accurate) or perhaps it can be xeroxed and pasted up to save redrafting of key sections. But leaving it wrong sends a poor message about the integrity of our work.

The strange thing about obsessing over technical detail is that it is often so much fun for students. Introducing a project, I typically describe with precision the tools we are about to use—where they were made, how they were made, where they were purchased, how much they cost, and where they fit in the hierarchy of quality. When we visit professionals in the field, my students' first questions are of- ten about the brands and qualities of tools and materials the professionals use. I have taken my students to an art supply store where they could peruse and purchase all levels of architecture tools and materials. I will often specify exactly which tools need to be used at which steps of a project—which paper for this draft, which pen for that draft—and it gives a tone of importance and clear structure to the process.

Unexpected Benefits

Details make a difference. In a study of geology, my students made polished stones at school using rock tumblers. At five weeks per batch, the process took a lot of patience and work. We bought jewelry-making supplies and made jewelry from the stones we had tumbled and from crystals we had collected during field work. The jewelry was sold at a store set up for the town, and the profits financed a multiday field trip to New York City. We wanted the jewelry to be of good quality, even if the components were low-budget, so we got advice from professional jewelry designers and we set up a quality-control system to ensure that anything going into the store was without flaw. In addition, students wanted workmanship to be guaranteed; all re- pairs would be free of charge. This was a kids' store, but it was vital to the kids that the merchandise be adult-quality.

After months of work making necklaces, earrings, rings, pins, and key chains, we were six hundred dollars in debt (my money), but rich in merchandise. Students were handling all the finances of the store, and at a certain point, they were faced with an important de-cision—pricing each item. This is the kind of detail that might have occupied ten minutes. Instead, it took three days, and I'm not sorry it did. The first two days were spent in dis-cussions and calculations of how to maximize profit. The higher the price, the higher our profit margin; but at high prices we might sell fewer items. What was the perfect balance? Through surveys of students and parents, the class finally came up with what seemed a rea-sonable mark-up. Then, on the third day, the discussion took a different turn. What was a reasonable amount to ask for items when our shoppers were often low- income children? How would kids from poor families feel if they were priced out of our store? To what extent was this a profit venture and to what extent was it a friendly outreach to the community? This was getting interesting.

At that point, prices were lowered, but it still didn't resolve everyone's concerns. Could we give discounts to families with less money? If so, which families should be eligible? Could they have access to the school's free-lunch list? (They couldn't.) If discounts were given, how could they be done in a manner so as not to embarrass the child or family?

The pricing policy that the class eventually came up with was quite different from what one would find in a typical store: any clerk working in the store was to be trusted to make the call on whom to give discounts to and what the discount should be. If there was a crowd at the store, the customer would be asked privately to return at a later time, when the discount could be given discreetly. In addition, a whole category of one-cent and five-cent items were added, especially for kindergartners who had no chance of buying a necklace for three dollars and fifty cents. The store grossed about fifteen hundred dollars, and there was no worry about loss of profit.

This jewelry store project is as much an example of deep thinking about substance as of obsession over detail. But my point is that the two are highly interdependent. My students could not have attained the same level of learning and of pride if they had failed to attend with great care to the many details of this work.

HIGH STANDARDS REQUIRE NEGOTIATION

People may assume that high standards must be rigid and unquestionable. Negotiation could only undermine them. For some aspects of school culture, such as safety, behavior, and respect, this is indeed the case. But what about best work? What represents the best effort and best work of each child, and how do we elicit it? If we hold to one rigid standard for all students when it comes to work, some students will achieve it with minimal effort and others may struggle earnestly and still fail.

Teachers in my school spend their evenings and weekends appraising the work of each student to determine just what level of effort that work represents. Is it acceptable at this level, or should it be returned for another draft? Like good teachers everywhere, we aspire to push each student to his or her maximum potential by refusing to accept work of poor effort.

Students know we do this. There is no secret teacher magic in our appraisals. When we return work, we conference with those students whom we feel need support or instruction, while others continue on project work. Students can choose to conference with us, and they can choose to contest our opinion. More than once this year, a student has approached me, often with eyes a bit teary, to explain that the work I would not accept represented much more effort than I had guessed. Often they provided explanations or evidence that were quite convincing. I applauded their self-advocacy.

What Is Negotiable?

With a class of all levels of ability, including substantial special needs, how do I hold everyone to the same high standard for final products? What is negotiable is not the quality of work, but the types of sup- port needed to produce this quality work. Perhaps a student will need teacher or computer assistance for one part of a project, or an ex- tended deadline or a waiver from certain components of the project. Quality is not negotiable, but scope can be. Students learn to self- advocate, not to avoid work but to ensure that they can realistically complete work with integrity. Almost every project we complete has mandatory components, which all students do, and optional components, which are clearly negotiable. This way students can work at different paces and still finish at the deadline.

This year a student with fine-motor problems ran into real difficulty: she had designed an enormous house as part of an architectural project and now was struggling with her drafting. Moreover, she had problems with the fragile paper we were using for blueprint work—all of her drafts were quickly torn. The solution she negotiated was to scale down the size of her house, which we agreed to, and to have her work taped down to a large drafting board, which she took home each night for homework.

During the course of projects or studies, the class as a whole often negotiates changes or additions in the project requirements or even whole new directions for the study. For example, I had intended to end our study of Deaf culture mid-year. My students simply re-fused. "How can you stop us in the middle of our learning?!" Too many of the aspects of the study represented ongoing relationships and ongoing language studies they were unwilling to give up. Not only did we decide to continue aspects of the study throughout the year, but this year a number of those students, now attending junior high school, are returning to my classroom in the evening for classes in American Sign Language taught by a Deaf woman with whom we established a friendship last year.

Another realm of negotiation for me is use of class time. I make plans for each day and plans for the week; but in project work, as in real life, things aren't always predictable. Time allotments for certain work must be lengthened, cut short, or changed entirely. Most often, I make these changes, but students learn that if they are polite and constructive in suggesting changes, their wishes will be given serious consideration. There may be a schedule full of different activities, but with an exhibition approaching, students plead for extended time to work on writing or drafting. If they can remain responsible, quiet, and focused, we often agree to this. There have been days in my class- room when students worked on blueprints for four or five hours straight, staying in the room for recess and only leaving briefly for lunch.

This negotiation of class-time use can also

be individual. While it is initially clear what is class work and what is homework and what a particular silent work time is set aside for, students learn that there is some room for individual negotiation here. If a certain draft of a piece of work is due Friday, a student may approach me and ask if she can work on this during the evening, as homework, and use the class time allocated for it to work on another aspect of the project. If she has proven herself responsible in this regard in the past, then she has good negotiating currency with me, and there is a good chance I will agree. Students watch this process and strive to be responsible enough to be allowed to plan parts of their own time also.

Earned Power

Clearly, this is a scary process for a teacher: it's hard enough to get kids to do work on time when deadlines and tasks are clear and rigid. What a mess it would be if students could negotiate these things! Strangely, teaching in the way I suggest isn't really as hard as it seems. Students are given power over their time and work only as they earn it, by showing that they can make responsible choices, that they can follow through on promises, and that they can plan their time wisely. These habits come quickly to some children, slowly to others. The level of teacher-imposed time structure that each student needs— and, indeed, wants—varies from student to student, and the teacher can adjust this accordingly, being frank in negotiations with the student.

I can't say that this is an easy process for me, or that I don't make mistakes in negotiating work with students. I sometimes find myself disappointed. Yet, every student wants to be trusted and respected, and even students I've taught with serious problems in emotional stability, behavior, or academic skills have worked very hard to earn the responsibility for managing their own time. Students often work twice as hard as normal during extra time they have negotiated; they want to prove their level of responsibility.

SCHOOL CULTURE MUST EXTEND BEYOND THE SCHOOL WALLS

At my school, we do all we can to bring the outside world in, in the form of local experts for our studies and community members to view and critique our work. And we also do all we can to get our students out into the community for field work, exploration, and service. The town support that my school enjoys could never have been built with- out this two-way outreach.

Field trips are an integral part of all major studies. Classes visit caves, mountains, sawmills, factories, laboratories, artist studios, retail stores, farms, hospitals, private homes, colleges, other elementary schools, and all kinds of sites. These trips are a chore to plan and often exhausting to manage. The payback, though, in student and teacher excitement and investment is well worth the trouble. Because we have no money for buses, all trips are accomplished with parent drivers. Almost all families have two working parents, so arranging field trips takes early and on-going effort to persuade parents to take a day off work to help with their child's education.

This tiring task has its hidden benefits. Students are prepared well for field trips—already possessing an impressive knowledge of the area under study—and parents accompanying us on trips are invariably delighted to see the students shine in this way, asking perceptive questions and exhibiting real interest. Parent loyalty to the classroom, the school, and its methods is forged during these occasions, and parents begin to feel an ownership of the school's goals. Parents, teachers, and students are all learners together. Most of all, these trips serve to put learning and knowledge clearly in the sphere of life, rather than simply in books and classroom studies.

Similarly, outside experts are brought into the classroom to speak with students whenever possible. These experts may be professionals in a field, sharing information in an area we're studying. They may be individuals coming in to critique or assist with artistic or academic skills. Or they may be people just coming in to share first-hand stories from their lives that bear on our work. Some of these "experts" are professors, crafts people, or business people; some are parents or siblings of students; some are even ex-students or students from other classrooms.

Once again, students are prepared thoroughly for each visitor so that they are not only polite but sophisticated and astute in listening and responding. Some experts are hard to line up for the first visit, but most are so pleased and excited by the level of interest and knowledge in the students that subsequent visits are easy to schedule. One professional Egyptologist, who I think had never presented to students below the college level, lowered her fee to visit us and planned to give a one-hour talk. She was so astonished at the students' passion for ancient Egypt and their knowledge of history and hieroglyphics that she stayed all morning, sharing stories and knowledge and helping students to translate hieroglyphics. She offered to guide us free of charge on an up-coming museum trip and stayed in touch all year. These outside experts serve to keep me fresh and excited as a teacher, and serve as models for students. They provide us with the vocabulary and concepts we need to critique our work in their field. They interest students in careers. And they allow students to watch me, as teacher, learn along with them.

We try to involve parents and families in school projects and studies as much as possible. Aside from field trips and giving presentations, parents, relatives, and neighbors are also invited to school regularly to listen to presentations by students or outsiders and to see exhibitions of student work. Families are encouraged to take an interest in projects, and their help is welcomed. Some projects are specifically designed to be community projects.

Bringing the community into our school

builds for us the foundation of support we need in our town. We are a strange and new-fangled school in a small, conservative town; we have no textbooks, no grades, and, in some rooms, no desks. We have won over the hearts of much of the town not because we talk a good line, but because the students do well in real-life measures of learning. They are capable and confident readers, writers, and users of math. They are strong thinkers and workers. They are polite and treat others well. We want people to see this, and we achieve it both by bringing the community in and by sending out of school each day students whose excitement in learning doesn't end at the school door.

TEACHERS NEED SUPPORT FOR GROWTH AS MUCH AS STUDENTS DO

In addition to working as a teacher, I also work as a carpenter. This has been a financial necessity for my family, given the salary limits of my primary career. In carpentry, the process of learning skills and expertise follows a sensible course. Carpenters do not learn their skill from a book, spend a month-long "internship" on a crew, then get certified as master builders ready to build a whole house by them- selves. You wouldn't want someone with such training building your house. Carpenters spend years acquiring skills on the job, being given successively greater levels of responsibility, and they serve an extended apprenticeship to experienced builders before they are considered experts.

Now, consider the teaching profession: teachers study education theory in books, typically spend a few months in a classroom (frequently with only one week of being in charge), and are then considered finished products of "teacher training." Following this training, they may immediately be placed in total charge of a classroom, with as much responsibility as they will have for the rest of their teaching careers. Whoever dreamed up this notion of teacher preparation must have been crazy.

In the absence of true apprenticeships, models, and on-the-job critique and support, most young teachers fall back on the memories of the teachers they had when they were in school themselves, not long before. They copy from memory and eventually build a repertoire of strategies to survive in that devastatingly scary and isolated first year. Most teachers cling insecurely to these early strategies for the next few years and even the next forty years. They make a fortress of their classroom, hoping to be left alone. They take pride in the success of individual students but feel always insecure about the success of the class as a whole, and react with inner terror when an observer enters their classroom.

Staff development is the cornerstone of building a culture of quality in schools. But such staff development cannot be purchased with a single mandate or structure imposed from above. Because it is ultimately a way of thinking, good staff development can only be purchased with respect for what teachers can accomplish together. There must be a wide range of opportunities and structures that allow and compel staff members to emerge from the fortresses of their classrooms and take responsibility to learn in different ways. Staff members must begin to work in teams to make important decisions; they must forge changes in school culture together. They must visit other classrooms and other sites and begin to see themselves as learners who are willing to give and accept critique. They must become reflective practitioners—teaching, learning, and researching in concert.

The same applies to administrators. Roland Barth points out in *Improving Schools from Within* (Jossey-Bass, 1990) that when the Harvard Principal's Center was founded as a place for school principals to share ideas and become active learners, fifteen hundred local principals were invited to attend the opening. Three showed up. Although interest picked up enormously later, it remains hard for principals everywhere to find the time and the commitment necessary to learn and grow within the profession.

It is a common thing to read in newspapers these days that students in Japan do well on tests, despite large class sizes. It is less common to read how well-respected and well-paid teachers in Japan are, how important education is in Japanese culture and families (to the point that mothers will come to school and take notes when their children are absent). And most significantly, it is less common to read that teachers in Japan only teach for sixty percent of their work day; the other forty per-

cent is given to the vital tasks of lesson preparation, meetings, critique, and staff development.
Sometimes I dream about what kind of teacher
I could be if had a third of my day to plan and
prepare, and not just nights and weekends.

CONCLUSION

Adult Work and Children's Eyes

THE TOWN WHERE I LIVE AND TEACH
is mostly forest. Only one quarter of the roads
are paved, and other than houses and small
barns, there is only a handful of buildings. Two
years ago, when we had to leave our school
building for a year so that an addition and re-
modeling project could be completed, there
was no building in town that could house us.
The closest site we could find was a old vacant
school building in a town half an hour away.

The town has limited resources, so the
move had to be a volunteer enterprise. The
complete contents of the school building were
packed up and loaded into cars, pick-up trucks,
and produce trucks loaned by a parent. The
planning, organization, packing, unloading,
and distribution were done by parents, students, ex-students, staff, and community members. There was a team of parents whose whole
job was to provide food for the sweaty hoards
of workers. The rented school building was in
disrepair, and staff worked with volunteer parents for a week to fix ceilings, paint walls, and
install blackboards. It was a wonderful testa-
ment to an extensive school culture. The spir-
it was that of a community barn-raising, and
had this been a Hollywood movie, there would
have been a playful montage set to music with
old and young working together to launch the
school year.

In real life, there were indeed Kodak moments and some laughter, but by the time school was supposed to open, the school staff was completely exhausted and overwhelmed. Our backs hurt; we were confused, short-tempered, and behind in all our planning. We sat in staff meetings in a trance—there was too much to do and too little time. It was clear that doing everything was impossible. Parts of the school, parts of the curriculum and program, just couldn't be ready in time.

At this point, the staff did something that I think most exemplifies the foundation of our school culture—we stepped back from our personal concerns and worries for a moment and tried to imagine what coming to this new school would be like for the children. What would be new and confusing, what would be safe and secure? What would provide order, continuity, sense, and immediate paths for positive behavior? What were the danger points? What would it be like for the less confident children—the youngest, the shyest, the students with physical or emotional difficulties? Our answers to these questions could guide us to the truly essential tasks.

In the process of answering them, it became clear to us just how much of our school culture was supported by routines and traditions built into the old school. Somehow we had to recreate those here, and we had to do it quickly. We had no choice but to spend time together hashing out new routines and traditions of arrival and dismissal, lunch and recess, school chores and rules, assemblies and exhibitions, places to display student work and to comfort troubled kids.

For example, we spent a tremendous amount of time discussing the bus ride. If there's one place where polite and kind behavior is apt to unravel, it's on a school bus. Anyone who has spent part of his or her childhood riding a school bus doesn't need much explanation in this regard. Given the move to a distant town, the staff was distraught by the notion of kindergarten children beginning their day spending a full hour in a potentially scary and confusing environment. During discussion, it was suggested that we expand on our existing partnership, which paired kindergartners with sixth graders, and have the sixth graders sit with the kindergartners on the bus and take care of them.

The staff supported this plan, and the teachers affected were given the complex task of matching the older and younger kids by bus route and personality. We then discussed the advantages and disadvantages of assigning bus seating to ensure a calmer ride; then we discussed strategies for assigning seats, giving limited choice, or simply creating new bus rules and constraints. The whole topic took hours, and this was just one of many routines we had to rework and rethink to provide a safe and kind environment in the new building. Sitting in these endless meetings, we complained at every juncture and individually planned secret strategies to sneak back to our classrooms and unpack boxes. We were used to maintaining routines, but it felt like we were starting from scratch and it took forever. But in the end, it made a real difference to the children that we obsessed about structures that made them feel safe and cared for; and it made a real difference to us to start the year with routines in place that made things feel calm, respectful, and cheerful.

Of course, new schools are not new forever, and they eventually develop stable traditions and schoolwide ethics that are self-sustaining. Still, maintaining a positive culture takes work, too— eternal work. No school can ever rest on reputation. Schools, my own included, are always prone to lose direction. Sometimes it's a small loss of direction: things just don't feel right, students seem less respectful and engaged, teachers feel dispirited. Sometimes it's a major crisis: direction has been lost for a long time, and the culture has become awful.

In either case, the key to recovery is the same, and it's not found in any book or mission statement. The key lies always in a close analysis of how children, all children, in the school are doing and in an honest appraisal of problems from the perspective of the children. Which ones are feeling adequately safe, supported, and challenged, and which are not? Which students are exhibiting courtesy and responsibility and which are not? And, perhaps most important, who has a sense of pride in the school? Is that pride universal?

Schools these days are very concerned with the self-esteem of their students, and rightly so. But self-esteem is not built from compliments. It is built from accomplishments of quality.

ABOUT THE AUTHOR

Ron Berger is Chief Academic Officer for EL Education, a nonprofit school improvement organization that partners with public schools and districts across America, leads professional learning, and creates open educational resources. He also teaches at Harvard Graduate School of Education, and founded the free website *Models of Excellence: The Center for High-Quality Student Work*.

The ideas in *A Culture of Quality* are expanded in Ron's subsequent book, *An Ethic of Excellence*, which brings further examples and description to the vision described in this book. Additionally, Ron has co-authored a series of books with his colleagues at EL Education: *Leaders of Their Own Learning*, *Transformational Literacy*, *Management in the Active Classroom*, and *Learning that Lasts*. He is a featured keynote speaker nationally and internationally on inspiring quality, character, and citizenship in students.

Ron was an Annenberg Foundation Teacher Scholar, and received the Autodesk Foundation National Teacher of the Year award. He was a public school teacher and master carpenter in rural Massachusetts for over 25 years.

ABOUT EL EDUCATION

EL Education is a leading national K–12 non-profit helping to build great schools in diverse communities across America.

For over 25 years, EL Education has been bringing to life an expanded vision of student achievement that includes mastery of knowledge and skills, character, and high-quality student work. EL Education promotes active classrooms: alive with discovery, problem-solving, challenge, and collaboration. EL Education drives results: teachers fulfill their highest aspirations and students achieve more than they think possible. EL Education students have both the capacity and the passion to build a better, more just world.

EL Education's expert educators work with schools (both district and charter) across 35 states, serving over 200,000 students and 16,000 teachers in our school network and multi-year literacy partnerships. Rigorous impact studies by Mathematica Policy Research demonstrate that EL Education's approach works: teachers significantly improve their craft and students achieve more, regardless of background.

Grounded in decades of in-depth work with educators, EL Education creates highly respected, widely distributed open educational resources, including the following: the world's largest collection of exemplary student projects; an acclaimed literacy curriculum that has been downloaded 8.7 million times and received the highest possible ratings from EdRe-

ports; inspiring instructional videos with over 1.3 million views; hundreds of free online resources; and best-selling education books.

EL Education was founded in 1992 by the Harvard Graduate School of Education in collaboration with Outward Bound USA, based on the belief that learning and achievement flourish when teachers and students are engaged in work that is challenging, adventurous, and meaningful.

ELeducation.org

ACKNOWLEDGMENTS

The school culture described in this book is a product of the remarkable dedication and talent of my colleagues at the Shutesbury Elementary School and the students and families of the town of Shutesbury.

This reflective essay was guided and improved by a number of educators, most notably Joe McDonald, then at the Annenberg Institute for School Reform, as well as Steve Seidel, Howard Gardner, and Vito Perrone of the Harvard Graduate School of Education.

I would also like to acknowledge the inspiration and fellowship of John Reid, who is featured in these pages and who was the most natural teacher I have ever known.

CPSIA information can be obtained
at www.ICGtesting.com
Printed in the USA
LVHW021025110620
657585LV00007B/503

9 781683 625629